W9-BHD-954

ANIMALS AT WORK
Animals
Making Homes

WORLD
BOOK

World Book, Inc.
180 North LaSalle Street
Suite 900
Chicago, Illinois 60601
USA

Produced for World Book, Inc. by Bailey Publishing Associates Ltd.

For information about other World Book publications, visit our website at **www.worldbook.com** or call **1-800-WORLDBK (967-5325).**

Library of Congress Cataloging-in-Publication data has been applied for.

Title: Animals Making Homes
ISBN: 978-0-7166-2734-0

Animals at Work
ISBN: 978-0-7166-2724-1 (set, hc)

Also available as:
ISBN: 978-0-7166-2747-0 (e-book)

Printed in China by Shenzhen Wing King Tong Paper Products Co, Ltd., Shenzhen, Guangdong
1st printing August 2018

Staff

Writer: Cath Senker

Executive Committee

President
Jim O'Rourke

Vice President and Editor in Chief
Paul A. Kobasa

Vice President, Finance
Donald D. Keller

Vice President, Marketing
Jean Lin

Vice President, International
Maksim Rutenberg

Vice President, Technology
Jason Dole

Director, Human Resources
Bev Ecker

Editorial

Director, Print Publishing
Tom Evans

Managing Editor
Jeff De La Rosa

Editor
William D. Adams

Manager, Contracts & Compliance
(Rights & Permissions)
Loranne K. Shields

Manager, Indexing Services
David Pofelski

Librarian
S. Thomas Richardson

Digital

Director, Digital Product
Development
Erika Meller

Digital Product Manager
Jonathan Wills

Manufacturing/Production

Manufacturing Manager
Anne Fritzinger

Proofreader
Nathalie Strassheim

Graphics and Design

Senior Art Director
Tom Evans

Senior Designer
Don Di Sante

Media Editor
Rosalia Bledsoe

Special thanks to:

Roberta Bailey
Nicola Barber
Francis Paola Lea
Claire Munday
Alex Woolf

A family of raccoons peeks out of its den in North America. Raccoons often make their homes in hollow logs, stumps, or trees.

Acknowledgments

Cover photo: © Gerald A. DeBoer, Shutterstock

Alamy: 5 (Robert Harding), 6 (Ivan Kuzmin), 9 (WILDLIFE GmbH), 10-11 (Raj Singh), 11 (Colin Varndell), 12-13 (Richard McDowell), 13 (Avalon/Bruce Coleman Inc), 16 & 26-27 (blickwinkel), 16-17 (Arterra Picture Library), 17 (Wildscotphotos), 19 (Dominique Braud/Dembinsky Photo Associates/Alamy), 20-21 (age footstock), 22 (Paulo Oliveira), 26 (GFC Collection), 27 (Mathew Jose K), 31 (Nature Picture Library), 33 (Paparazzi by Appointment), 34 (Manfred Grebler), 35 & 43 (imageBROKER), 36-37 (Reinhard Dirscherl), 38-39 (WildPictures), 40 (William S. Kuta), 42 (F1online digitale Bildagentur GmbH), 42-43 (Hira Punjabi). **Shutterstock:** title & 41 (Mauricio S Ferreira), 4 (Tappasan Phurisamrit), 6-7 (I. Grasbergs), 7 (tahirsphotography), 10 (Spreewald-Birgit), 14 (Tom Reichner), 14-15 (Zoltan Tarlacz), 15 (Kevin Wells Photography), 22-23 (Barsan Attila), 25 (Dutourdumonde Photography), 29 (Simon Greig), 30-31 (Ludmila Yilmaz), 32-33 (Tom Goaz), 34-35 (Chase Dekker), 37 (davidtclay), 38 (Mps197), 39 (Maksimilian), 45 (JeremyRichards).

Contents

Introduction

Think about the place where you live. Your house or apartment protects you from bad weather, such as rain or snow. It keeps you and your family warm during cold weather and cool during hot weather. Your home is also the place where you keep your belongings.

Animals build houses for many of the same reasons people do. They create safe spaces to sleep, raise their young, or even to store food. These places range from shelters used only for an afternoon nap to houses used generation after generation.

Most animals build their houses themselves. Many creatures build nests and dens from materials they find nearby—grass, twigs, feathers, mud, fur, or hair. Some dig under the soil or into wood. Others build houses underwater, attach their shelters to plants, or even create wearable houses! Spiders weave webs; they use their houses to trap **insects.** Some animals build a huge shared house for their community.

Some animals are not builders. They simply find a ready-made home, such as a hole in a tree, a crack in a rock, or a sheltered cave. Some room with other animals or steal their homes. Other **species** live on other creatures.

Not all animals have a permanent place to live. Fish are always on the move, living in different places. Worms live in water or soil, eating small plants and animals or rotting things wherever they are. Insects and small snakes use temporary shelters— caves, rocks, plants, or logs—and then move on.

Some animals live in a home **range,** an area where they can find food and shelter. The size of the home range depends on the size of the creature. Elephants and lions need a large area to roam around to find enough food to eat. Some animals have a **territory,** an area they fiercely defend from others.

A parrotfish rests in a temporary home, tucked into a small rocky space.

In this book, you will read about the many different kinds of houses animals use for protection and shelter. You will learn about some amazing feats of animal engineering.

A yellow-bellied marmot sits at the opening of its burrow. Burrows dug by marmots for hibernation may be up to 23 feet (7 meters) deep.

A Cozy Nest

Animals commonly build nests for shelter from **predators** and bad weather, to attract a **mate,** and to raise young.

BIRDS' NESTS

Most birds make a nest in a tree, on a riverbank, on the ground, or on a ledge for laying **eggs** and caring for their chicks. Nests can be simple. In the Pacific Ocean island country of New Zealand, the kiwi (a chicken-sized bird that cannot fly) lays its eggs in a hole in a riverbank. Other birds build their nests from leaves, twigs, and moss.

Some birds make huge structures. The white stork builds its giant nest on rooftops and chimneys. It forms a platform with large branches and adds smaller branches and dried leaves, using mud to make solid walls so the eggs will not fall out. It fills the nest with small leaves and moss to make it soft and cozy. Storks also use human materials they find lying around, such as plastic, paper, and even clothes. Having gone to so much trouble, stork pairs use the same nest every year, making repairs and improvements as needed.

American cliff swallows make their nests from pellets of mud. Each pellet is collected in the bird's beak, and added to the nest. Some nests may contain over 1,000 mud pellets.

A white stork sits on its nest perched on top of a chimney.

Nests for show

Male birds of many **species** of weavers that live in Africa build elaborate hanging nests to attract **mates** as well as to raise their young. A male strips shoots and green leaves to make threads, and ties them to a branch. At the loose ends, he weaves a ring, big enough for him to pass through. This is the entrance. The bird then weaves blades of grass through the threads to complete the nest, including a long entrance tube too narrow for any **predators** to enter. To show off his fine creation, he hangs upside down from the nest, calling and fluttering his wings to encourage a female to visit. If no female likes his nest, he tears it down and builds a new one.

A weaver shows off his fine nest.

A Beautiful Bower

Bowerbirds live in Australia, New Guinea, and other nearby Pacific Ocean islands. The males make bowers (special areas or rooms) to attract females. They build these large, tent-like structures from natural materials gathered nearby: sticks, grass, vines, and moss.

The design of the bower depends on the **species** of bowerbird that is building it. Some species make simple mats or platforms on which to show off. Others gather sticks of the same size to make two parallel walls, sometimes with an arch over the top, building their avenue over a round twig mat. Still others build a tower of twigs around one or two saplings (young trees). A male may reuse its tower, building it taller each year. Such a tower can reach several feet or a few meters in height! Some species add a soft moss lawn around the tower. Other species build huts that can also reach large sizes.

Not content with just building a structure, many bowerbirds decorate their bowers and lawns with brightly colored objects. A bird finds attractive things from nature—petals, berries, feathers, seeds, and flowers. If they start to fade, he replaces them with fresh ones. Waste materials from humans come in handy, too—metal cans, plastic, and bottle tops. Bowerbirds love bright, sparkling objects. Some bowerbirds even paint the walls of their bower. They chew up plants and mix the chewed plants with charcoal to make paint. Some even use leaves or a chewed-up twig as a paintbrush—a rare example of tool use in an animal.

When a female bowerbird arrives to examine the male's work, he bows, dances, and sings to court her. The bower is all for show. Once a female has accepted a **mate,** she lays their **eggs** in a simple nest a short distance away in a tree.

A SATIN BOWERBIRD decorates his bower with blue objects, including plastic bottle tops.

A BED FOR THE NIGHT

Chimpanzees and gorillas move to a new place to eat every day. They make a fresh nest every time they sleep, even for daytime naps. Gorillas live in the thick rain forests of central Africa. Every morning, the leader takes his troop to a new place to eat leaves and fruit. At sunset, each gorilla builds a nest from folded branches and leaves, usually on the ground, but sometimes in a tree.

Like gorillas, chimpanzees move around to find food and make a new bed every night. Parents teach their young how to build their nests safely in the trees. The youngsters learn that they should build their bed near the top of a tree, at least 15 feet (4.5 meters) from the ground. Taking branches that are soft and flexible, the chimps weave them to make a platform, covering the nest with leaves for warmth. Sleeping in the high branches protects the chimps from **predators** and pesky **insects** and **parasites.** In hot weather, it is cooler up in a tree than on the ground. When it is chilly, chimps can wrap themselves in leaves to keep warm.

Smaller **mammals** build nests, too. Squirrels make nests in trees, also for protection from predators. Field mice collect dried grass to make little nests that are hidden away under logs, or in the undergrowth.

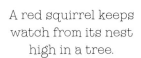

A red squirrel keeps watch from its nest high in a tree.

Mountain gorillas sit in their nest in the Volcanoes National Park, Rwanda.

A winter bed

Some **species hibernate** in the winter, entering a sleeplike state so they do not need to eat when food is hard to find. Their body temperature lowers and heartbeat slows so they need little energy. The dormouse is a little **rodent** that looks like a small squirrel. In cool climates, it builds a nest on the ground under leaves for warmth. It sleeps for much of the winter, only waking once in a while on warm days to nibble some of its stored food.

A dormouse in hibernation. Dormice build up reserves of fat in their body to get them through the hibernation period.

Burrows, Dens, and Lodges

A burrow is a tunnel or hole, dug by an animal to make a home. Some creatures dig burrows to use for a long time. Others dig a new burrow each time they need one. Dens are hollow chambers (rooms) in the hillside, rocks, or caves. The beaver is a master builder, constructing its complex lodge in a river.

BURROWS

Some birds, frogs, **insects, mammals,** snakes, spiders, and worms dig burrows underground, ranging from a simple hole to a complex network of tunnels and chambers. Burrows protect animals from **predators** and extreme temperatures found at the surface. Some burrows are a source of food: there are roots, pieces of dead plants and animals, and other burrowing animals underground.

Found in moist soil around the world, some earthworms make permanent burrows deep in the ground. They eat dead plant material they find there. As they dig, they loosen and mix the soil and enable air to enter, which helps plants to grow.

THE RIGHT BODY FOR THE JOB

Many **reptiles** dig burrows to get away from the heat or cold and to hunt their **prey.** Snakes, some lizards, and other burrowing creatures do not have arms or legs so they slip more easily through soil and sand. Some lizards dig underground by ramming their heads into the soil. They have thick skulls to protect their heads. Shield-tailed snakes, which live in southern India and on the nearby island of Sri Lanka, have pointy heads for digging through soil and smooth scales for sliding easily through burrows.

A burrow with a trap door

Trap-door spiders live in warm climates, including the southern and western United States and tropical places. They are named for their clever hunting method. A trap-door spider covers the opening to its burrow with a trap door made from mud and silk, attached with silk hinges. (Spider silk is a material which looks like thread that the spider pushes out of its body.) The spider waits patiently behind the door. When an insect goes by, the spider quickly opens the door, grabs the prey, and pulls it into the burrow.

The opening of a trap-door spider's burrow is made from mud and silk.

A lizard comes out of its sand burrow in western Australia.

PRAIRIE DOG BURROWS

Prairie dogs are large ground squirrels that live on the North American prairies. Using their strong claws, they dig long tunnels to form huge underground towns.

Each burrow is carefully designed. Around the opening is a mound of soil that stops floodwater from entering the burrow. The raised opening makes a good place for prairie dogs to watch for approaching **predators,** such as snakes and coyotes.

A coyote hunts for food on the prairie. Prairie dogs use their burrows to hide from such predators.

There are several chambers just below the surface where prairie dog guards listen for attackers, too. The **rodents** also dig deep tunnels up to 16 feet (5 meters) below the surface. Here, they build chambers for storing food and sleeping. During the day, the prairie dogs leave the burrow to look for food, but run back to safety if they sense danger. At night, they sleep in the deepest chambers.

Around 500 animals may live in a single town, and it is strictly organized. Prairie dogs live in family groups called coteries (*KOH tuhr eez*) or clans, and each clan has its own **territory.** Members of the clan chase away prairie dogs from other family groups. The clans are grouped together in wards, and all the wards together make up the town.

Built for digging

Badgers' bodies are well adapted for digging, and they can quickly build complex burrows to avoid **predators.** Their huge front paws have strong claws for loosening earth. They make long digging movements with their front limbs, while their rear legs push back the dirt as they work. For protection from flying soil, the badger has an extra see-through eyelid that it can close to protect its eyes from dirt, and it has stiff hairs in its nostrils and ears to keep dirt from flying in.

This badger digs with its large paws and strong claws.

Prairie dogs keep watch at the entrances to their burrows.

DOWN IN THE DEN

Wild dogs, foxes, and bears dig a den or find one in the landscape. In the chilly Arctic Islands of Canada, Arctic foxes make dens in the few places where the ground thaws in summer. It takes a lot of energy to dig a den, so the family uses the same one each year. After the pups are raised, a daughter takes over the family home from her parents. Some dens may even be hundreds of years old.

Most bears make a den for their winter sleep. (Bears do not truly **hibernate:** their body temperature does not drop and they can wake up quickly.) They make dens under fallen tree trunks, rocks, or roots or in caves. Grizzly bears build a large mound of dirt in front of their den to seal it. Some bears also bring brush, leaves, or grass to make their home cozy and nestlike.

ESTIVATION

Some animals hide away in their dens to **estivate**—shelter from hot, dry weather. In the Sonoran (*suh NOHR uhn*) Desert of northwestern Mexico and the southwestern United States, temperatures can soar to a scorching 120 °F (49 °C). A rattlesnake out and about in temperatures above 110 °F (43 °C) will die. Deep in its den, its breathing and heart rate slow down to reduce the need for water and food. When rain arrives and temperatures cool, the snake begins to move about again.

A western diamondback rattlesnake at the opening of its den in the southwestern U.S. state of Arizona.

A brown bear cub comes out of its den into the snow.

An Arctic garden

Arctic fox dens make lots of waste. The mother and her litter of eight to ten pups defecate (*DEHF uh kayt;* get rid of solid bodily waste) in the area around the den. Scraps of leftover food may also litter the entrance. This waste material is full of **nutrients** that make the soil good for growing plants. Natural gardens of beautiful Arctic flowers grow around the den.

An Arctic fox cub sits close to its den.

A CLOSER LOOK

A Feat of Engineering

Beavers are large **rodents** that live in rivers and lakes near forests. Beaver families build houses called lodges in the water for protection from wolves and other **predators.**

If the family of beavers settles in a river or stream, it builds a dam. First, the beavers find a place where the water is not too deep. In the nearby forest, they cut down small trees by gnawing (chewing and biting) through the trunks. A beaver has huge incisors—sharp front teeth—for this work. Its lips close behind the teeth so water cannot enter its mouth while it is carrying branches underwater. The beavers use the tree branches to build a dam, pushing them into the mud in the river bottom to make the foundations. On top they pile logs, branches, and bark to slow the flow of the water and create a pond upstream where the water is still.

The beavers build a lodge in which they live. They make a mound with logs and stones, sealed with mud, in the lake or pond to form an island. They build a dome-shaped roof from branches, dried leaves, and grass. The beavers cover this structure with mud and moss. They make a chimney in the roof so air can move freely.

Inside the mound, the beavers dig out two rooms. One is for drying off after swimming and the other is a bedroom. The adults share it with their young.

The beavers make two underwater openings in their lodge. One is steep for going in and out. The other is gently sloping, for bringing in branches, bark, and leaves to eat. Only the surface of the water freezes in winter, so the openings to the dam stay open for the beavers to go in and out.

To keep unwelcome visitors away, the beavers make a stinky fence around the riverbanks with castors—small piles of mud mixed with smelly stuff they give off from scent **glands.** Other animals stay away from the area because of the bad smell of the castors.

A NORTH AMERICAN BEAVER sits on the edge of its lodge, surrounded by water.

Ranges, Caves, and Webs

Many animals have a home **range**—an area where they normally live. Some defend their home range from other creatures. A home range that an animal defends is called a **territory.** Other animals find ready-made houses, while spiders spin their webs between natural objects.

HOME RANGES AND TERRITORIES

In their home range or territory, animals find all their food, resources for survival, and places to rest, breed (make more animals like themselves), and hide from enemies. Some creatures stay in their home range or territory for just a day. Others stay there for months, years, or their whole lives.

The size of the range depends on the resources available there. If the area is rich in food, then the range does not need to be large to support an animal. If meals are hard to find, animals need to roam a larger area. Elephants have a home range that changes at different times of year. These large animals need lots of space: individual ranges are from 5.4 up to 1,204 square miles (14 to 3,120 square kilometers)—almost the size of the northeastern U.S. state of Rhode Island.

WARNING INTRUDERS

The **savannas** of **sub-Saharan Africa** are home to many kinds of animals, including elephants, lions, and rhinoceroses. Lions live in a large group of several families called a pride. They live in the same territory for generations and guard it fiercely from other prides. If you hear a lion roar, it is advertising that it owns the area. The roar can be heard at least 3 miles (4.8 kilometers) away, so rivals know to stay away!

Marking territory

Rhinoceroses have their own way of marking their territory. They spray urine (liquid bodily wastes) on trees and bushes, and scatter dung (solid bodily wastes) around the area. Other rhinos will pick up the scent and keep out. If they enter, the resident rhinos chase them off their territory. If an outsider enters a rhino's territory, it will charge. Rhinos have poor eyesight, so they are quick to charge at possible outsiders, if just to get a better look at (and whiff of) them!

A lion stands guard over his territory in the Maasai Mara National Reserve, Kenya.

TROGLOXENES – MAKING USE OF CAVES

Caves stay cool in the summer and warm in the winter. Many animals make use of this feature, spending parts of their lives in caves. Birds and other creatures nest in the mouths of caves. Bats sleep and breed in caves. Bears may also make their dens in caves. These animals are called **trogloxenes** (*TRAWG luh seenz).* They spend some time in caves but must leave to find food or **mates.**

TROGLOBITES – PERMANENT CAVE RESIDENTS

Troglobites (*TRAWG luh byts),* on the other hand, are animals that spend their entire lives underground in caves. Some **species** of fish, **reptiles,** worms, and spiders are troglobites. Adapted to the dark conditions, they frequently have small eyes or none at all, because eyes are useless in total darkness. Many troglobites are pale in color. They would stand out above ground, but since there is no light in caves, their colors do not matter. Cave snails have thin white or see-through shells, and smaller eyes than regular snails. Some crayfish (small **arthropods** related to lobsters that live in fresh water) that live in caves are pure white and totally blind. Troglobites use other senses than sight for finding their **prey;** they usually have very sharp senses of hearing and touch. Some **insects** that live in caves have **antennae** twice as long as their bodies for feeling for prey.

TREES AND HOLLOWS

A ready-made house may be far smaller than a cave. In wooded areas, such **mammals** as raccoons and skunks set up house in hollow logs, tree stumps, or holes in the ground. Where there are not enough trees, such animals might nest in long grass, unused burrows, or human-built structures.

Cellar glass-snails are found on rocks and in crevices in caves such as this one in Portugal.

Bats hang upside down by their back legs, with their toes locking on to the surface of the rock so they do not fall.

A tiny breeding pond

The gladiator tree frog makes his own tiny pond from a bigger one, using his legs to form a mud wall to enclose it. Or he may simply use the hollow from an animal footprint. The female lays her **eggs** in the pool. The male guards the eggs and young until the tadpoles become little frogs and hop out of the pond.

Homes as Traps

Spiders build webs between trees and other objects. The sticky silk threads the spider makes form a trap as well as a home. The spider can move freely around its web. But when **insects** fly into it, they get stuck and become food for the spider.

Webs can be flat or in the shape of a tube or funnel. They are mostly vertical (up-and-down), but some are horizontal. Most common is the orb web, which you can spot in parks and gardens.

To make an orb web, the spider makes a frame with four sides, attached to trees or other objects. Then it builds threads from the middle to the outer edge—like the spokes of a wheel. It finishes by making a sticky spiral thread from the outer edge round and round to the center. Spiders make different types of silk. It is all incredibly strong, but the strongest silk is for the "spokes" stretching across the web. Weight for weight, it can be five times stronger than steel. (That means if you took spider silk the same weight as a piece of steel, the silk would be five times stronger.)

The golden orb weaver spider of Australia makes some of the largest webs on Earth. This huge spider, as wide as a human hand, makes a golden-colored web up to 3 ½ feet (1 meter) in diameter, hanging between trees or posts. The largest golden orb weavers can even trap birds in their webs.

In Waitomo Cave, New Zealand, glowworms (**larvae** of a type of gnat) spin sticky silk threads from the cave ceiling. They drop **mucus** along the webs, which makes them glow in the dark with a blue light. Insects are attracted to the light and become stuck in the thread. When an insect gets trapped, the glowworm reels in the thread and eats it.

The web of the GOLDEN ORB WEAVER spider is a huge structure.

Living in a Colony

Bees, wasps, and ants live in **colonies,** building complex hives and nests for storing food, raising young, taking shelter from the weather, and hiding from **predators.** Many bird **species** gather in huge colonies at breeding time.

WASPS AND BEES

Wasps hang their nests from tree branches or buildings. They build their nests from a paper that they make themselves. To make their paper, worker wasps scrape pieces of wood from a tree and chew them into a soft pulp. They shape the wet pulp into the walls and cells of the nest. Each cell has six sides, which allows each one to share a side with six others without creating any empty spaces in between. When the pulp dries, it becomes solid.

Honey bees create their hives in caves or tree hollows. Worker bees make sticky beeswax, chewing it and mixing it with saliva to make the wax soft. They form six-sided cells, which fit together to form a honeycomb.

UNDERGROUND ANT HAVEN

Leafcutter ants build complex nests with tunnels, chambers for making food and dumping garbage, and chimneys. The biggest chambers on the edge of the nest are for waste. The ants bring leaves to the food chamber. After chewing the leaves, they mix them with saliva and feces (*FEE seez;* solid bodily waste) to make food for growing **fungus** to eat. To keep the air fresh, the ants build chimneys. Fresh air enters through the side of the nest, and stale air is forced out of the chimneys on top.

A leafcutter ant carries a leaf back to its nest.

Living glue sticks

Tropical weaver ants form colonies in trees. Hundreds of worker ants haul leaves and position them with their edges together. Other workers use sticky silk from the **larvae** to bind the leaves. They hold the larvae and move them back and forth along the edges to let out the silk. The larvae are living glue sticks!

Weaver ants make their nest by sticking together the leaves of a tree.

A CLOSER LOOK

Termite Mounds

In warm areas of the world, termites live in **colonies** with millions of individuals and work together to build huge nests. The above-ground portion looks like a giant slab of mud. In Africa and Australia, mounds can be up to 20 feet (6 meters) tall. Inside are thousands of tunnels and chambers where the termites live and raise their young. Like leafcutter ants (see page 26), many **species** grow their own **fungus** to eat inside the colony.

As in other **insect** colonies, the workers do most of the building. They choose a place for the colony near the trees and bushes the termites eat. The workers build the nest using soil, saliva, and dung of large animals. Once the nest is built, the workers clean and repair it and build new tunnels as the colony grows.

If you happen to be lost, a termite mound can help you find your way. Termites know the path of the sun across the sky. They always build their mounds with the broad sides facing east and west, and the narrow sides facing north to south. This helps to keep the temperature inside the mound comfortable. In the early morning, the sun shines on the eastern side and warms up the mound. At midday, it shines on the top, but only a narrow edge is in sunlight, so the nest does not get too hot. As the sun sets in the west, it warms the western side, giving some heat but not so much that the termites bake inside.

More animals than just termites can be found inside the mound. Many other **arthropods** live there, including beetles, caterpillars, flies, and scorpions. Lizards and snakes may also make use of the shelter, and birds may dig into the mounds to make their nests.

BIRD COLONIES

About one in eight birds **species** nests in a **colony.** Albatrosses, auks, gulls, and other seabirds form colonies, as do some wetland birds, such as herons. Some songbirds, such as weavers, some blackbirds, and swallows also live in groups.

FEEDING AND BREEDING

Birds mostly gather when it is time to breed. All birds need to lay their **eggs** on land—and it has to be the right kind of place. Water birds choose places that land **predators** cannot reach: tall trees, reed beds, islands, or cliffs. Since only some places are suitable, the good locations become extremely crowded. For example, flamingos make nests in a particular kind of mud, so they breed at just a few places. One east African colony has more than one million birds.

How do such big groups of birds manage to find enough food? Birds form their colonies close to good food sources, and large groups can work together to feed more efficiently than individuals. African penguins herd fish in the open sea by swimming around the groups and pushing them together into a tight circle so it is easier to catch them. In wetlands, American white pelicans also herd fish, driving them toward the shallows where they can pick them off.

PROTECTION FROM PREDATORS

For defending eggs and young, there is safety in numbers. In the colony, there are many members to watch for predators and tell others of danger. Flocks of birds can even chase some predators away, such as an attacking crow.

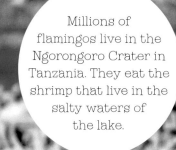

Millions of flamingos live in the Ngorongoro Crater in Tanzania. They eat the shrimp that live in the salty waters of the lake.

The downside of community life

Colonies have some downsides, too. They attract the attention of predators, which hunt the young, weak members, and those at the edge of the group. Diseases spread quickly, food can run out, and natural or human-caused disasters, such as an oil spill, can destroy a whole group.

Oil spills can devastate groups of animals. These brown pelicans have been taken to a wildlife center to be cleaned.

Living on Others

There are many fascinating examples of creatures that live on other animals or plants. The guests may help their **hosts,** or at least do no harm. Others are **parasites** that seriously harm the health of their hosts or even kill them.

MUTUALISM: HELPING EACH OTHER

The clownfish is a small, brightly colored fish. It lives in a sea anemone (*uh NEHM uh nee).* Like a jellyfish, the anemone has stinging tentacles that protect the clownfish from **predators.** The clownfish is covered with a thick layer of **mucus** to prevent it from being stung itself. In return for its home, the clownfish cleans the anemone's tentacles and attacks other fish that might eat the sea anemone.

Acacia (*uh KAY shuh)* ants do not need to build nests— they live in bullhorn acacia trees, which give them both shelter and food. The ants live inside the acacia's large, hollow thorns. The queen lays her **eggs** inside the thorns, and the workers care for the young there once they hatch. The acacia plant provides sugary sap and fleshy leaf tips for the ants to eat. In turn, acacia ants defend the tree from animals that try to eat the leaves or fruit. Soldier ants sting any animals that land on it. They even remove vines and other plants that try to grow on their home. This living arrangement is an example of **mutualism** (*MYOO chu uh lihz um):* two **species** that need each other to survive. The ants cannot live anywhere else, and the tree suffers if it has no ants living on it because its leaves get eaten.

A clownfish makes its home in a sea anemone.

Symbiosis—living together

Symbiosis (*sihm by OH sihs, sihm bee OH sihs*) describes any two species that live together. There are three different kinds.

- **Parasitism (*PAR uh sy tihz uhm*):** one species lives at the expense of the other, the host.

- **Commensalism (*kuh MEHN suh lihz uhm*):** one species benefits but the other one is not badly affected.

- **Mutualism:** both species benefit, such as acacia ants and the acacia tree.

A parasitic wasp has laid its eggs on a caterpillar. When the eggs hatch into larvae, they will eat the insides of the caterpillar.

COMMENSALISM

Sometimes, one animal can benefit from a **host** in a way that neither seriously helps nor hurts the host. Such a **symbiotic relationship** is called **commensalism.** Barnacles (*BAHR nuh kuhlz)* are a kind of **arthropod** that lives in oceans. Young barnacles go through a series of free-swimming **larval** stages, but after a while they stick to an object and grow a hard case around their bodies. Sometimes, they stick to large ocean animals, such as whales and sea turtles. The barnacles filter food from the water, so they benefit from their hosts swimming to places with lots of food. On the other hand, the huge animals that barnacles attach themselves to hardly notice them.

PARASITES OUTSIDE AND INSIDE

In most symbiotic relationships, one **species** harms or even kills its host. This is called **parasitism. Ectoparasites** live outside their host and eat its skin, blood, or feathers. Mosquitoes, fleas, and leeches are ectoparasites that drink blood. Some ectoparasites are specially adapted to keep from being felt by their hosts. Leeches have a chemical in their saliva that stops the host from noticing the bite and killing the leech.
Endoparasites are harder to notice until they cause harm. They live inside or on their host and eat it or take its **nutrients.** They include roundworms and flatworms.

Flukes are parasitic flatworms. Some cause schistosomiasis (*SHIHS tuh soh MY uh sihs),* a tropical disease that can kill people. These flukes live in snail and **mammal** hosts. The fluke's **eggs** hatch in water, and the larvae swim about until they find a snail. They grow in the snail, then return to the water and search for the skin of a mammal. People who wade or swim in the water may be infected. The fluke pierces their skin, attaches itself with suckers, and drinks their blood.

Two leeches feed on a horse's leg.

You can see the barnacles that live on this humpback whale as it feeds in Monterey Bay, off the coast of California.

From host to host

Blood flukes can have two or more hosts: snails, fish, **insects,** plants, and humans. One blood fluke, called the green-banded broodsac, lives in the eye tentacle of a snail. It changes the snail's behavior so that it does not hide when it senses danger, so a bird is likely to spot the infected snail and eat it. After the snail is eaten, the fluke's eggs hatch out in the bird.

The green-banded broodsac is a parasitic flatworm that lives in snails. It infects the snail's eyes, making them swell up.

Mobile Homes

Some creatures build houses around their bodies to guard against **predators** wherever they go, to protect **eggs,** or for defense while they change into their adult form.

SAFE IN A "SLEEPING BAG"

Parrotfish are large, colorful fish, with teeth like a parrot's beak. They live in coral reefs in the Indian and Pacific oceans. Most fish move about during the day and sleep at night. But nighttime is dangerous: sharks prowl the reef, eating sleeping fish. The parrotfish forms its own protection. At night, its skin makes a large amount of **mucus,** which forms a bag around the fish, sealing in its scent. A shark cannot smell it to track it down. The parrotfish can sleep safely in its mucus "sleeping bag" until daybreak. It is also good for avoiding infection. Researchers have shown that if a parrotfish's covering is removed, many more **parasites** can infect its skin and blood. Making a sleeping bag every night is worth the effort.

A FOAMY NEST

A female gray foam-nest tree frog nests on a branch overhanging water, where it is hard for predators to reach her. She gives off a watery fluid from her body, whips it into a foam with her back legs, and lays her eggs in it. Male frogs arrive and join in, thrashing their back legs to make a huge foamy nest. They **fertilize** the eggs, which are protected inside the nest. When the tadpoles hatch, they wriggle out of the foam and tumble into the water.

A parrotfish sleeps safely in its mucus "sleeping bag."

In a chrysalis

A caterpillar builds its own house around itself when it is time to change into a butterfly. The caterpillar attaches itself to a branch using silk. Its skin splits apart to reveal a covering called a chrysalis (*KRIHS uh lihs*) underneath. The hardened chrysalis does not move, but, inside, the caterpillar's body is changing into the wings, legs, and body of a beautiful butterfly.

A chrysalis protects the caterpillar while it turns into a butterfly.

LIVING IN A CASE

Caddisflies are mothlike **insects** that live in and around water. Most caddisfly **larvae** live in lakes, rivers, and other bodies of fresh water. They look like caterpillars and would make a nutritious meal for **predators** such as fish and other **arthropods** that live in the water.

Some caddisfly larvae weave their own mobile homes, called cases, to protect their squishy bodies. The larva makes silk from **glands** in its mouth to glue together pebbles, shells, leaves, and sticks from the river bottom, forming a strong case shaped like a tube. The case is open at the top and bottom so the animal's head and thorax (middle section of the body) stick out at the top.

The larva case is like a suit of armor for the caddisfly, protecting it from predators.

The larva can move around without leaving its house by pulling the case along with its **abdomen.** The case also **camouflages** the larva; it is hard for **predators** to spot the creature peeping out of its home. When the larva grows large enough, it anchors the case to the ground, seals itself inside, and changes into an adult caddisfly, much in the same way a caterpillar changes into a butterfly (see page 37).

Camouflage

Many living things are colored to match their background—they are camouflaged. Being camouflaged helps them to hide from predators or the **prey** they are chasing. Houses can be camouflaged too. Many birds build nests in colors that match the landscape to make it harder for predators to find them. Researchers offered male zebra finches a choice of nest-building materials. Some matched and some did not match the cage walls. The birds mostly chose materials that matched the background color of the cage, showing that they tried to blend their nests in with the landscape.

The nest and eggs of the European snipe are perfectly camouflaged to blend in with the surroundings.

The caddisfly builds its protective case from different materials. This case is made from pieces of stone.

Animal Squatters

Some animals steal the houses of others while they are away, and others move into empty houses.

HOME STEALERS

The gopher tortoise of eastern North America makes intricate burrows with long tunnels that shelter it from direct sunlight and heat during the day. When the tortoises go out at night to find food, raccoons, snakes, lizards, and foxes sneak into the comfortable burrows to sleep while the owners are away. These animals usually do not bother the gopher tortoise, although they may eat any **eggs** or baby tortoises they find there.

Some burrowing owls do not bother to build their own homes, preferring to live in burrows built by other animals. Sometimes these are old, empty burrows. But burrowing owls are known to move into the burrows of such animals as prairie dogs. If the prairie dogs try to defend their burrow, the owl eats them. In some areas, it looks like burrowing owls must steal the **rodents'** homes to survive. In the United States, farmers may kill prairie dogs because they blame them for competing for food with sheep and cattle. In places where many prairie dogs have been killed, burrowing owl populations have fallen, too.

A gopher tortoise outside the opening of its burrow in Estero, Florida.

Tuataras make bad roommates

The **reptile** called the tuatara lives on only a few small islands of New Zealand. Tuataras are pretty large reptiles, 2 feet (60 centimeters) long. Some tuataras use the breeding burrows of seabirds, such as shearwaters and petrels, for shelter. The burrows make perfect homes because they are full of bird droppings, which attract the beetles and **insects** that the tuatara eats. The housemates keep different schedules: shorebirds move about during the day and sleep at night, while tuataras search for food at night and sleep during the day. They do not always get along, though. Tuataras will eat unguarded eggs and chicks, so seabird parents often try to drive out the invaders. Sometimes, tuataras will even eat adult birds!

A burrowing owl protects its home.

SECOND-HAND HOMES

Some creatures generally wait until another has left its home before moving in. Many **species** of hermit crabs live on the ocean floor or along the seashore, while other kinds live on land. With its soft **abdomen** and no shell of its own for protection, a hermit crab looks for an empty shell to use as a house. The hermit crab's favorite house is an empty shell from a sea or land snail. It eases its abdomen into the shell and holds on to its new home with a pair of legs. Its other legs and claws are covered in a tough material, so they stay outside the shell. If the hermit crab senses danger, it crawls into the shell and blocks the opening with its claws.

MOVING HOUSE

As a hermit crab gets bigger, it may outgrow its shell. It searches its **habitat** until it finds a larger suitable shell and crawls in, leaving its old home behind. A smaller crab may in turn take over this shell. If there are not enough empty snail shells around, hermit crabs fight over the existing ones. A crab may also try to rob a live snail—killing it in the process—if it cannot find a suitable empty shell. Some hermit crab species have alternative homes. They may live in the tubes of plant stems, broken coconut shells, pieces of wood, or human-made objects.

A hermit crab may use a human-made object in place of a shell if it is sturdy and of the right size and shape.

Shell mates

Some hermit crabs have a **mutualistic** relationship (see pages 32–33) with other creatures called anemones. These species carry anemones around on their shells. The anemone waves its tentacles around to catch food as the crab carries it through the water. This is useful for the crab—those stinging tentacles keep **predators** away. The hermit crab even coaxes the anemone onto its new shell when the crab moves. In turn, the messy crab makes scraps for the anemone to eat.

A hermit crab with its anemone partners on its back.

This hermit crab has moved into an empty shell.

A New Home for Wildlife

Humans have pushed out entire animal populations by taking over their **habitats.** But in places that people have given up, animals have moved back in. Over the course of just a few decades without humans around, **ecosystems** can recover, even in the face of war and extreme pollution.

Pripyat is a ghost town in the eastern European country of Ukraine. In 1986, the Chernobyl nuclear power station exploded, giving off a dangerous poisonous cloud that spread over Ukraine and nearby parts of the countries of Russia and Belarus. It was too hazardous for people to live in the area, so the government ordered all the people out of the town of Pripyat. Wild boar, wolves, elk, and deer moved in. Rare animals also appeared, including the European bison and lynx (a type of wildcat). In 2014, brown bears were spotted in Pripyat. They had not been seen in the area for more than 100 years.

For the past 50 years, few people have entered the demilitarized zone (area where no armies can enter) between the east Asian countries of North and South Korea. Created in 1953 after a war between the two countries, the zone is thought to be home to more than 2,700 different **species,** including such **endangered** creatures as the Siberian musk deer, Amur leopard, and the rare Amur goral—a kind of wild goat.

The Falkland Islands are a group of tiny islands in the South Atlantic Ocean, about 320 miles (515 kilometers) east of the South American country of Argentina, but owned by the United Kingdom. During a 1982 war between the United Kingdom and Argentina, the Argentinian army laid thousands of mines (buried bombs) along the coast near the capital, Stanley, to prevent further British attack. Penguins now live there—they are too light to set off the mines.

The white sandy beach in Yorke Bay on the Falkland Islands is home to MAGELLANIC PENGUINS. It is too dangerous for people because of the land mines that were laid there in the 1982 war.

DANGER MINES

Glossary

abdomen the rear part of an arthropod's body.

antenna (plural antennae) a long, delicate sense organ, or feeler, found on the heads of various invertebrates, including insects. Invertebrate animals do not have a backbone.

arthropod a very large group of invertebrates that includes insects, arachnids, and crustaceans. Invertebrate animals do not have a backbone.

camouflage the natural coloring or form of an animal that enables it to blend into its surroundings, making it difficult to see.

colony a group of living things of one species that live together or grow in the same place.

commensalism a symbiotic relationship in which one species benefits and the other is not affected.

ecosystem a system made up of a group of living things and its physical environment, and the relationship between them.

ectoparasite a parasite that lives on the outside of or near its host.

egg a female sex cell, or the structure in which the embryo develops, usually outside the mother's body.

endangered a species or other group of living thing that is at risk of going extinct (dying out).

endoparasite a parasite that lives inside of its host.

estivate to spend hot, dry periods in an inactive state. Breathing, heart rate, and other body processes slow down.

fertilize to join sperm from a male with egg from a female so that a young animal develops.

fungus (plural fungi) a living thing that usually grows on plants or on decaying matter. Yeast and mushrooms are fungi.

gland an organ in an animal's body that secretes (gives off) chemical substances for use in the body or for release into the surroundings.

habitat the place where a living thing usually makes its home.

hibernate to spend the winter in a state like deep sleep. Breathing, heart rate, and other body processes slow down.

host a living thing that is either harmed or not affected in a symbiotic relationship.

insect one of the major invertebrate groups. Insects have six legs and a three-part body. Invertebrate animals do not have a backbone.

larva (plural larvae) the active, immature stage of some animals, such as many insects, that is different from its adult form.

mammal one of the major vertebrate animal groups. Vertebrate animals have a backbone. Mammals feed their offspring on milk produced by the mother, and most have hair or fur.

mate the animal with which another animal partners to reproduce (to make more animals like the two that are mating); the act of mating, when two animals come together to reproduce.

mucus a thick liquid that is produced in parts of animals' bodies.

mutualism a symbiotic relationship in which both species benefit.

nutrient a substance that is needed to keep a living thing alive and help it grow.

parasite a living thing that lives on or inside another living thing, such as an animal or plant, and gets its food from it.

parasitism a symbiotic relationship in which one species benefits and the other is harmed.

Find Out More

predator an animal that hunts, kills, and eats other animals.

prey an animal that is hunted, killed, and eaten by another.

range the area in which a species can be found.

reptile one of the major vertebrate animal groups. Vertebrate animals have a backbone. A reptile has dry, scaly skin and breathes air. Snakes, crocodiles, and lizards are all reptiles.

rodent a mammal with front teeth made for gnawing hard things.

savanna grasslands with widely scattered bushes and trees.

species a group of living things that have certain permanent traits in common and are able to reproduce with each other.

sub-Saharan Africa the part of Africa south of the Sahara Desert.

symbiosis, symbiotic relationship a relationship between two species from which at least one benefits.

territory an area of land or water controlled by an animal or group of animals, which they defend from other animals.

troglobite an animal that lives its entire life in a cave.

trogloxene an animal that lives part of its life in a cave.

BOOKS

Animal Homes (Young Architect) by Saranne Taylor (Crabtree Publishing, 2014)

Animals: A Visual Encyclopedia by DK Publishing (DK Children, 2012)

How and Why Do Animals Build Homes? by Bobbie Kalman (Crabtree Publishing, 2014)

How Animals Build by Lonely Planet Kids (Lonely Planet Kids, 2017)

WEBSITES

Animal Homes
http://thekidshouldseethis.com/tagged/animal-homes
Check out videos about different kinds of animal homes.

Animal Homes
http://www.kidport.com/RefLib/Science/AnimalHomes/AnimalHomes.htm
Links to different animal homes, including caves, trees, nests, ground, webs, and water homes.

Habitat: Animal Homes
https://www.pbslearningmedia.org/resource/nat15.sci.lisci.anihome/habitat-animal-homes/#.WdzXvBTbgzI
Short videos about how animals build their homes.

PBS: Nature
http://www.pbs.org/wnet/nature/animal-homes/11674/
A series of three videos about nests, animal architecture, and colonies.

Index